Together Forever

Written and illustrated by
Jeannie St. John Taylor

Abingdon Press
Nashville

Together Forever

ISBN 10: 0-687-33582-5
ISBN 13: 978-0-687-33582-4

07 08 09 10 11 12 13 14 15 16–10 9 8 7 6 5 4 3 2 1

Printed in China

To my niece Carolyn Taylor,
my father Clare St. John,
and my late pastor Ron Mehl.

Someday I'll hug you again.

Once upon a time a young girl's brother died. Sadness fell on her like rain. Tears wet her cheeks. Nothing brought her joy; not the mountains and trees,

not the flowers,

not the sunsets.

On her brother's birthday, she wandered
into the garden alone. "I miss him so much," she whispered.
"I wish I could have just five more minutes with him." But
she knew it could never happen. Sinking onto a bench under
a rose-covered arch, she fell into a deep sleep.

In a dream, she heard her brother's giggle and felt his soft touch. The girl laughed and cried and hugged her brother. They spent the day playing together again,

twirling through wildflowers
and swinging on the old tire swing,

blowing
bubbles,

capturing ladybugs
and frogs,

and climbing
the gnarled pine tree
and munching wild raspberries.

Near evening, they leaned against the tree house railing, gazing across the valley at the purple mountains. They watched fireflies flicker above the grass.
"Isn't it beautiful?" the young girl sighed.
"Not as beautiful as heaven," her brother said.

They climbed down the ladder,

and the sister tickled her brother's nose with
a lilac blossom. "Doesn't it smell wonderful?"
she asked. "Heaven smells better," said the boy.

For a long time they sat in silence on a mossy rock beside the creek. Then the sister whispered, "I wish you could come back and live with me again." The little boy smiled and hugged his sister's neck. "I'd rather wait for you in heaven."

They sat together
for a while longer.

He kissed her cheek one last time.
The dream ended and the sister awoke.

The sister plucked a rose and drifted down the pebbled path. A breeze stirred the oak leaves above her head. Brushing a tear from her cheek, she turned toward the sunset, letting the orange and pink glow bathe her face. "It may be a long time before I stop feeling so sad," she said aloud. The memory of her brother stirred the beginnings of a smile deep in her heart. "But I know I'll see my brother again . . . in heaven."

"Then we'll be together forever."